CULTURE IN ACTION

Terrifying Tales

GHOSTS, GHOULS, AND OTHER THINGS
THAT GO BUMP IN THE NIGHT

Liz Miles

www.raintreepublishers.co.uk
Visit our website to find out more information about Raintree books.

To order:

☎ Phone 0845 6044371

🖺 Fax +44 (0) 1865 312263

🖳 Email myorders@raintreepublishers.co.uk

Customers from outside the UK please telephone +44 1865 312262

Raintree is an imprint of Capstone Global Library Limited, a company incorporated in England and Wales having its registered office at 7 Pilgrim Street, London, EC4V 6LB – Registered company number: 6695582

Text © Capstone Global Library Limited 2011
First published in hardback in 2011
The moral rights of the proprietor have been asserted.

Edited by Louise Galpine and Diyan Leake
Designed by Victoria Allen
Original illustrations © Capstone Global Library Ltd 2011
Illustrated by Randy Schirz
Picture research by Hannah Taylor
Originated by Capstone Global Library Ltd
Printed in and bound in China by CTPS

ISBN 978 1 406 21719 3 (hardback)
14 13 12 11 10
10 9 8 7 6 5 4 3 2 1

British Library Cataloguing in Publication Data
Miles, Liz. – Terrifying tales : ghosts, ghouls, and other things that go bump in the night. – (Culture in action)
809.9'3375-dc22
A full catalogue record for this book is available from the British Library.

Acknowledgements
We would like to thank the following for permission to reproduce photographs: Alamy Images pp. **12** (© United Archives GmbH), **15** (© United Archives GmbH), **24** (© Andrew Jenny); The Art Archive p. **11**; Corbis pp. **14** (Bettmann), **25** (Rune Hellestad); Getty Images pp. **13** (David Sacks); istockphoto pp. **21** (© Max Homand), **22** (© Csaba Peterdi); The Kobal Collection pp. **5** (Warner Bros), **16** (Universal), **17** (Maverick Films), **18** (Warner Bros), **20** (Renown); Photolibrary p. **6** (Barbara Heller); Rex Features pp. **4** (© Paramount/Everett), **8** (SNAP), **23** (Alex Macnaughton), **26** (Marty Hause); Smart Pop/BenBella Books p. **7** (http://www.benbellabooks.com); © Tate, London 2010 p. **10**.

Cover photograph reproduced with permission of Getty Images (Stone+/Chris Strong).

We would like to thank Scot Smith and Jackie Murphy for their invaluable help in the preparation of this book.

Every effort has been made to contact copyright holders of material reproduced in this book. Any omissions will be rectified in subsequent printings if notice is given to the publisher.

Author
Liz Miles is an experienced author of non-fiction and fiction for children, with over 60 published titles.

Literacy consultant
Jackie Murphy is Director of Arts at a centre of teaching and learning. She works with teachers, artists, and school leaders internationally.

Contents

Some words are printed in bold, **like this**. You can find out what they mean by looking in the glossary on page 30.

Scary stories

"The moonlight cast shadows across the moors. Weeping, the lonely orphan heard the distant howl of a wolf. She walked faster. Hairs rose on the back of her neck … there was someone, or something, in the shadows. And it was following her."

Writing like this make us feel uneasy, but the **suspense** is exciting. We turn the page to find out what happens next. Scary tales and horror stories have always been popular. Many of today's writers, such as R. L. Stine (who wrote the Goosebumps series) and Holly Black and Tony DiTerlizzi (authors of The Spiderwick Chronicles), have become famous for keeping their readers in suspense.

Supernatural

Frightening tales are filled with ghosts, **zombies**, **vampires**, and other strange beings. Horror and ghost stories are often grouped into the literary **genre** called **supernatural fiction** or dark **fantasy**. *Supernatural* describes anything that exists outside the natural world. Ghosts and similar beings are supernatural because scientists cannot prove that they exist or explain what they are.

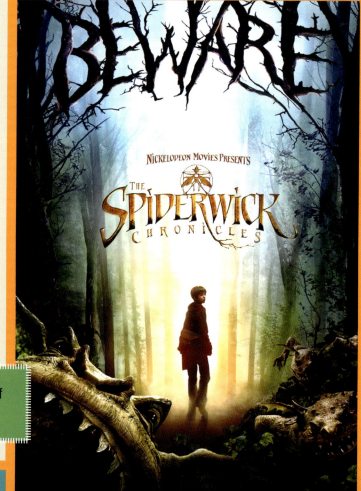

This is a poster of the film of The Spiderwick Chronicles.

What readers expect

Every good story creates suspense. A horror writer creates suspense and fear. The author describes likeable **characters** and creates almost-believable horrific beings. When these are put together in the same room, the reader starts to worry for the characters. This book looks at some of the best supernatural stories and how writers try to scare us senseless.

Ghosts

People may say that they don't believe in ghosts, but they may still be afraid of them! The skill of an author is to make you feel that way – scared of something, even if it is not real.

Inspired!

Scary tales of the **supernatural** have been around for thousands of years. The creepy parts in ancient **myths** and traditional **folktales inspire** many of today's horror writers. Writers have also based their stories on accounts of what people think they have seen in real life.

Monsters and ancient myths

One of the first stories ever written describes a terrifying, supernatural monster. "The Epic of Gilgamesh" was written over three thousand years ago in Sumer (now called Iraq). It describes "a terror to human beings", whose "mouth is death" and "breath is fire".

Ancient Greek myths include evil beings like the people-eating Minotaur, which has a man's body and a bull's head.

Such deadly monsters are just as popular today. The American author Rick Riordan brings ancient Greek monsters to life in his series about a boy called Percy Jackson. Percy has to fight monsters such as the one-eyed Cyclops from ancient Greece.

This image of the Greek Minotaur dates back to two and a half thousand years ago.

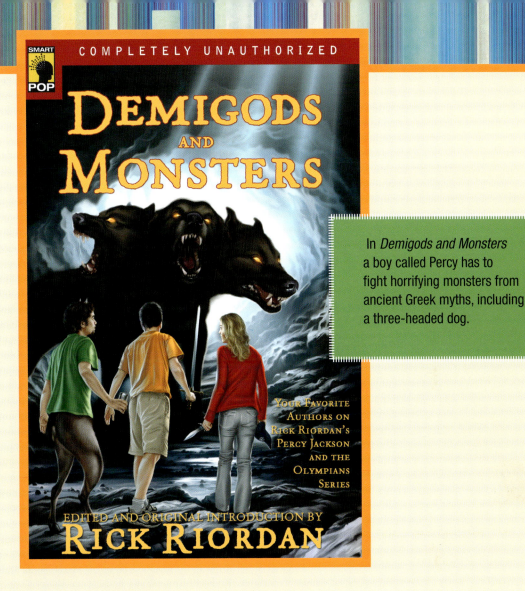

In *Demigods and Monsters* a boy called Percy has to fight horrifying monsters from ancient Greek myths, including a three-headed dog.

Ghouls and folktales

Ghouls appear as mythical creatures in Arabian folktales, such as in the collection of tales from as long ago as the 700s called "Thousand and One Nights" (or "Arabian Nights"). Ghouls live in old buildings and feed on dead bodies.

Today, ghouls appear in stories written all around the world. American adult horror author H. P. Lovecraft describes them as clambering "vile things" that live underground. English author C. S. Lewis lists ghouls along with other horrible creatures as serving a witch in The Chronicles of Narnia series.

Ghostly accounts

Pliny the Younger (AD 61–c.113), a writer in ancient Rome, wrote the earliest known ghost story. It was about a philosopher in Athens who heard rattling chains. An old man in chains beckoned him into the garden, and then disappeared! A hole was dug on the spot – and a skeleton was found there!

Shapeshifters

Tales of **shapeshifters**, such as werewolves, were common in times when wild animals often killed farm animals, or people. Werewolves are said to be men who change into wolves at night (usually when there is a full moon).

The Beast of Gévaudan (probably a wolf) killed more than 50 people in France between 1764 and 1767. It was shot with a silver bullet and paraded through the town.

Man or wolf?

In 1591, Peter Stubbe was put to death for being a werewolf in Germany. Fearing torture, he admitted to killing and eating 13 children.

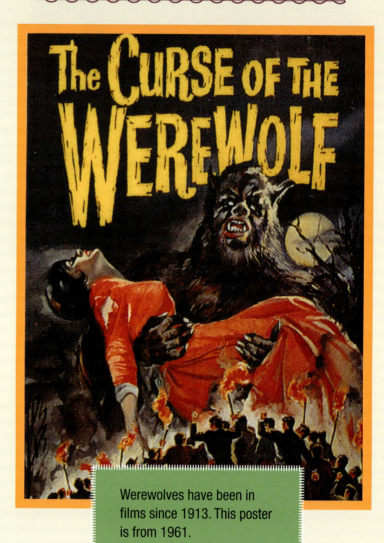

Werewolves have been in films since 1913. This poster is from 1961.

Horror art

Create a front cover for a new horror story about werewolves called *Werewolf Terror*. There is a **synopsis** of the book below to help you.

Synopsis

Children start to go missing at Tom's boarding school, Grangers High. Tom follows his teacher, Mr Simms, into the woods one night. He discovers the horrifying truth – Mr Simms is a werewolf!

Steps to follow:

1. Look through this book for examples of scary images. Think about why they look scary. This might give you ideas for your cover.

2. Decide on the picture for your book cover. Where is Tom? What is in the background?

3. Decide on what text to include, such as the title and author name.

4. Draw a rectangle 130 x 200 millimetres (5 x 8 inches) in black ink for the cover outline.

5. Experiment with your design. When you are ready, sketch your text and illustration in pencil. Try different **fonts** and think about the colours you want to use.

6. Add colour to finish the cover.

7. Hang your creation for others to see. Are they scared?

   Remember: The cover must be eye-catching, and look scary.

Gothic settings

The phrase *horror stories* was first used in the 1960s, but scary novels and poems were popular well before then. The word **gothic** was sometimes used to describe them. The first gothic novels had creepy castle settings with dark corridors and locked doors.

Creepy castles

The first gothic novel came out on Christmas Eve in 1764. It was called *The Castle of Otranto, a gothic story* and was by Horace Walpole, an English writer. The book was popular and the beginning of a new **genre**.

The Castle of Otranto has lots of gothic ingredients: a castle setting, a gory beginning (a groom is "dashed to pieces" when a giant helmet falls on him), and a ghost scene.

Castle of Otranto

This pen-and-ink drawing shows the ghost scene from *The Castle of Otranto*.

Scary seas

The gothic genre includes poems as well as stories. The English poet Samuel Taylor Coleridge used the sea as a ghostly gothic setting. In "The Rime of the Ancient Mariner" (1798), the mariner (sailor) and his ship get lost in sea fog and ice. After the mariner shoots a bird called an albatross, a ghostly **spirit** haunts the ship. The crew begin to die from lack of water. Another ship appears but not to rescue them – it is a ghost ship with two spirits on board: Death and Life-in-Death!

Modern tales

Modern scary stories are set in all kinds of gothic-style, frightening places, such as old mansions and graveyards. A grim house features in Book 1 of *A Series of Unfortunate Events* (1999) by Lemony Snicket (an American whose real name is Daniel Handler). Three orphans are made to live in Count Olaf's house. It has closed blinds, a tall and dirty tower, and a front door carved with the image of an eye. The reader knows the children will be miserable in this "terrible place".

The Addams family, featured in creepy **fiction** in books, films, and television programmes, live in an old mansion. The setting is especially scary because it is right next to a cemetery.

In a 1991 film, the Addams family live in a mysterious mansion on Cemetery Lane.

Even the trees are dangerous in *Shadow Forest*.

Frightening forests

Deep, dark woods are places where children should *not* go – or so many fairy tales and other stories tell us. In the children's novel *Shadow Forest* (2007) by Matt Haig, orphans Samuel and Martha are forbidden to enter the forest at the bottom of their garden because "no human who enters there returns alive". But Samuel enters to find his sister. Among the horrors he faces are an evil Shadow Witch and trees that crush people to death.

In a series called The Spiderwick Chronicles, by Holly Black and Tony DiTerlizzi, three children have to move from New York City, USA, to a falling-down mansion in the middle of a forest. Here, they discover a frightening world of "faeries".

Monsters, vampires, and witches

Monsters, **vampires**, and witches are scarier if you are in the same room as them. In stories, the reader comes face to face with these terrors by seeing them through the eyes of a **character**.

Nightmare

Mary Shelley was a young author who was at a gathering at the house of the poet Lord Byron one stormy night. She and other guests could not leave because of the thunderstorm. They spent the evening reading ghost stories to each other. Later, Lord Byron suggested they each write a ghost story. Mary had a nightmare in which she dreamt of a "hideous" **phantom** that started to come to life. It gave her the idea for Frankenstein's monster.

Mary Shelley wrote many books and stories, but *Frankenstein* is the most well known.

Zombies — the walking dead

Zombies feature in many stories, films, and real-life accounts. In the West Indies, there are tales of **sorcerers** digging up dead bodies and bringing them back to life. It is said that the sorcerers force the zombies to work for them as slaves.

Frankenstein has been made into many films, including this one from 1931. Here, Boris Karloff stars as the monster.

The book is about a scientist, called Frankenstein, who uses dead body parts to build a living "man". Frankenstein's creation turns out to be a vile-looking monster. Although gentle, everyone runs away from the monster or tries to kill him because he looks so horrific. Lonely and angry, the monster seeks revenge, and becomes a murderer.

Shared feelings

Mary Shelley lets the reader share Frankenstein's feelings of terror. We see the horror of the monster through Frankenstein's eyes. He describes its "yellow skin" and "straight black lips". We share Frankenstein's "breathless horror" and "disgust".

Bram Stoker's *Dracula*

Suspense makes us want to read on. *Dracula* is about vampires and has plenty of suspense. Part of the suspense in a vampire book is in waiting for the vampire to attack!

The Irish author Bram Stoker wrote *Dracula* in 1897. It is written in the form of three people's diaries. At first, we follow events through Jonathan Harker's eyes. Early on in the book, Harker describes Count Dracula, and the reader starts to worry!

The Dracula story has been made into many films, including this one from 1931.

Killing vampires

As in many vampire **myths**, Count Dracula sucks the blood of an innocent person, Harker's friend, Lucy. Lucy then dies and becomes a vampire herself. Professor Van Helsing, a vampire expert, helps Harker to kill Count Dracula. They drive a wooden stake through the vampire's heart. Other vampire stories give different ways of killing vampires, such as letting the sun shine on them, or shooting them with a silver bullet.

21st-century vampires

Vampire stories are still popular today. A best-selling series for young adults is The Saga of Darren Shan (2000). The hero is a vampire's assistant. The popular Twilight series by Stephenie Meyer is about a teenager who falls in love with a 104-year-old vampire!

The Twilight stories have been made in films starring Kristen Stewart and Robert Pattinson.

A flesh-eating prince

Bram Stoker's Count Dracula was based on a real prince who ruled in Romania in the 1400s. Prince Vlad III liked to impale people on stakes and eat the flesh and blood of his enemies. His nickname was "Dracul", which means "the devil".

Witches

Witches or devilish women are often the fearsome focus of books, especially children's stories.

The German Brothers Grimm wrote many tales of witches in the 1800s. In "Hansel and Gretel" a witch wants to fatten up a boy and eat him.

Best-selling witches

The usual image of witches is of women who wear pointed hats and ride broomsticks. Modern authors, such as Roald Dahl, make them scarier. In Dahl's story *The Witches*, pretty women turn out to be masked, grizzly, child-hating witches. Dahl describes them as "shrunken and shrivelled" with "scabby bald heads".

Roald Dahl's witches are among the most horrific. This is from the 1990 film based on his book *The Witches*.

18

Night with a vampire

Write and perform the part of a very frightened person.

Steps to follow:

1. Imagine that you are staying the night in Count Dracula's castle. It is time for bed and you are in your room. You have met the Count and are frightened. You have realized that he is a vampire!

2. Write down your feelings of horror by answering the questions below. You can then use your answers for a dramatic performance.

- What makes the castle frightening?

- How did you feel when you met the Count? What did he look like?

- You are in your candlelit bedroom. What might happen next?

- Can you hear any noises? What or who do you think is coming closer?

3. For your dramatic performance, imagine you have a mobile phone. You ring a friend to get help. Use your answers to explain to your friend why you are so scared.

Remember to use:

- tone of voice (whispering, high-pitched)

- pace (slow, fast)

- dramatic words (pick the best from your answers).

Ghosts, ghouls, and demons

Stories about ghosts are very popular. Some ghost stories hold a message or try to teach the reader a lesson. Other ghost-story writers just hope to frighten their readers!

Teaching with fear

A Christmas Carol, by the English writer Charles Dickens, became one of the most popular Christmas stories. Yet, it is about ghosts. The plot teaches the reader and a **character** called Scrooge about the meaning of Christmas.

On Christmas Eve, Scrooge, as always, is miserable and mean. A ghost called Jacob Marley appears. He is tied up in chains and cash boxes because, like Scrooge, he was mean in his lifetime. Marley warns Scrooge to avoid the same fate. Three **spirits** visit Scrooge. They make Scrooge look at himself in the past, present, and future. He sees how nasty he has become, and how he will die a hated man.

In this 1951 film of *A Christmas Carol*, Scrooge is terrified at the sight of his own grave.

On Christmas morning, Scrooge wakes and finds he has been given the chance to change. He seizes this opportunity and is generous and cheerful.

The Black Cat

The American writer Edgar Allan Poe wrote a short but terrifying tale about the horrific effects of being addicted to drinking alcohol. The alcoholic **narrator** becomes a horrible person. He kills his pet cat, but the cat returns in a **supernatural**, ghostly form. The narrator then kills his wife, and the mysterious cat makes sure the police find out.

A way with words

Poe is famous for his simple but grisly descriptions, such as: "It was night, and the rain fell; and falling, it was rain, but, having fallen, it was blood." (from *Silence, A fable*)

Black cats often feature in scary stories.

21

Graveyard setting

Today, as in the past, writers use ghosts and **ghouls** to scare us. Neil Gaiman's award-winning children's novel, *The Graveyard Book*, is a good example.

Gaiman sets an eerie graveyard scene early on in the book. The reader is asked to imagine the stones, tombs, and vaults in the light of a half-moon. The author describes the rattling of padlocked gates and spike-topped iron railings.

Through the eyes of …

In the story, a boy called Bod finds refuge in the graveyard after he wanders in as a toddler. The reader experiences the graveyard terrors through the eyes and ears of Bod and his friend, Scarlett:

"The noise began all about them, a rustling slither, like a snake twining through dry leaves … Scarlett made a noise that was half gasp and half wail, and Bod saw something, and he knew without asking that she had seen it too …"

The Graveyard Book won a prize called the Newbery Medal in 2009.

Suspense and horror

Suspense is set up from the first sentence in *The Graveyard Book*: "There was a hand in the darkness, and it held a knife." A man called Jack kills Bod's family with the knife. Later we discover that Jack will come after Bod, too.

Horror comes in the form of ghouls. Bod meets horrible ghouls with "teeth so strong they can crush any bones".

Terrified or horrified?

Terror and horror are different. Terror is when you feel fear — for example, if you see a ghost. Horror is the disgust you might feel for a flesh-eating ghoul. Gaiman offers both for a double dose of excitement.

Neil Gaiman has made a successful career out of terrifying his readers!

Bestsellers

Horror and terror are found in lots of modern literature, both for children and adults. Authors have become famous for terrorizing us, the readers. Some adult horror is so gruesome that lots of adults prefer not to read it!

King of Horror

American writer Stephen King is one of the most successful writers of horror. His books are for adults. His first novel, *Carrie*, came out in 1974. It was so scary and violent that it was banned from some schools in the United States. Lots of his books have been made into adult horror films, and have earned him a lot of money.

Stephen King's home in Bangor, USA, has the perfect gate for a writer of scary stories.

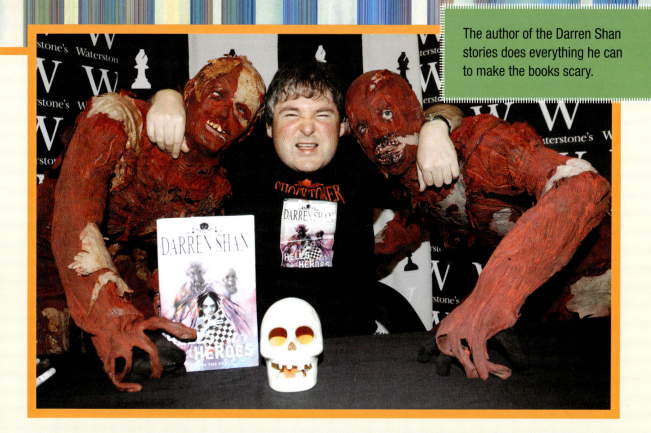

Fact or fiction?

The Saga of Darren Shan is a top-selling series for older children about a young boy, called Darren Shan, who goes to a strange **freak** show. There, Darren enters a dark world of **vampires**.

The **narrator** is Darren and no other name appears on the cover. It is as if the story is fact, which makes it seem even more frightening. Of course, it is really **fiction**. The author's real name is Darren O'Shaughnessy and he wrote his first novel when he was 17 years old.

Horror debate

It is difficult for adults to know what children should and should not read. Everyone wants to choose their books for themselves. But very frightening tales can cause nightmares. Some people believe that reading violent novels can make the reader violent. What do you think?

Skeleton hero

There are many successful authors writing horror and **gothic**-style stories for children. Derek Landy wrote the Skulduggery Pleasant series. These books feature a smartly dressed skeleton detective, who battles with an ancient evil force. Landy was paid £1 million upfront for the first book in the series!

Prize winner

Prize-winning American author R. L. Stine shot to fame when he wrote his Goosebumps series for children in the early 1990s. Stine started writing when he was nine years old.

Stine says his books are popular because they are "like a rollercoaster ride, you know what you are in for when you get on, there are lots of thrills, lots of crazy twists and turns, and it lets you off safe at the end".

R. L. Stine writes scary stories and encourages others to write, too. This photo shows him speaking at a book festival in 2004.

Bumps in the night

Terrifying tales are often made into films. With a friend, create the music and sound effects for a scary scene.

Steps to follow:

1. Make up a film scene. Choose from:

- a person running through a moonlit graveyard (owl, wolf, ghostly howl, scream)

- a person exploring castle rooms (creaking doors, echoing footsteps, ghostly howl, whispering voices)

2. Borrow a music player and a tape recorder or other sound-recording machine. Make sure you know how to operate them.

3. Gather together objects such as boots with noisy soles and instruments (for example, percussion instruments, a kazoo, cymbals, or any noisy objects you can knock or rub together). Find some eerie music on a CD. Experiment with your own voice.

4. Plan the order of your sounds, and then record them.

5. Re-record until you are happy with your scary film soundtrack.

Timeline

*c.*1500—1000 BC	"The Epic of Gilgamesh" is written, which tells of a **supernatural** monster
AD 61—*c.*113	Pliny, an ancient Greek philosopher, lives during this time and writes the earliest known ghost story
1764	The first **gothic** novel comes out: *The Castle of Otranto, a gothic story*, by English writer Horace Walpole
1812	The first collection of fairy tales by the German Brothers Grimm is published
1817	The ghostly poem "The Rime of the Ancient Mariner" is published. It is written by Samuel Taylor Coleridge, an English poet who often suffered from nightmares.
1818	The author Mary Shelley writes *Frankenstein*, the man-made monster
1843	*A Christmas Carol* by English author Charles Dickens is first published
1849	Edgar Allan Poe, writer of horrific tales, is found lying in a gutter. No one knows what happened to him. He dies in hospital.
1897	Bram Stoker writes a story about the blood-sucking **vampire** *Dracula*
1974	Stephen King's adult horror novel *Carrie* is published. It is about a disturbed girl who can move objects with her mind.
1983	*The Witches,* by prize-winning English children's author Roald Dahl, is published

1992	R. L. Stine begins his popular Goosebumps series with a book entitled *Welcome to Dead House*
1997	*Harry Potter and the Philosopher's Stone*, the first title in the Harry Potter series by J. K. Rowling, goes on sale. The series is so popular that the author becomes a multi-millionaire.
2000	A vampire's assistant is the lead **character** in the first of a horror series for older children, The Saga of Darren Shan
2003	*The Field Guide* (Book 1 of the Spiderwick Chronicles) is published
2006	*The Lightning Thief* (Book 1 of the Percy Jackson series) is published
2007	*Shadow Forest* by English writer Matt Haig is published. Its scary forest setting is in Norway.
	The first title in the Skulduggery Pleasant series by Derek Landy is published
2009	Neil Gaiman wins the Newbery Medal for *The Graveyard Book.* The medal is an American award for the most distinguished children's book.

Glossary

character person or creature in a story. The main character in the Harry Potter series is Harry Potter!

fantasy type of story with imaginary creatures or people. You could put unicorns and gnomes in a fantasy book.

fiction stories; tales that are made up

folktale old tale based on stories told through the ages. Many stories today are based on folktales.

font type of lettering that is a particular style. Times New Roman is an example of a font.

freak person, animal, or plant that is abnormal or deformed; it is usually considered to be an unpleasant way to describe anything

genre type of story. People label books according to their genre, such as fantasy, horror, and science fiction.

ghoul evil spirit or demon. The word *ghoul* was once used instead of "grave robbers".

gothic style of writing that focuses on dark and mysterious places and characters

inspire encourage a person to do something. Good books might inspire you to write.

myth ancient story. Myths are often about gods, goddesses, and strange beings.

narrator person who tells a story. In some stories one of the characters is the narrator.

phantom ghost; supernatural being

shapeshifters imaginary creatures that change shape. Some shapeshifters, such as werewolves, change into animals and then back into human form.

sorcerer person who practises magic

spirit supernatural being

supernatural not natural or normal, impossible to explain in a scientific way

suspense feeling of anxiety about what might happen next. Suspense makes the reader turn a page.

synopsis story put in just a few sentences. Some authors plan a story by writing a synopsis first.

vampire blood-sucking being. Vampire bats suck blood, and they do exist.

zombie dead person who has been brought back to life

Find out more

Books

My Favorite Writer: R. L. Stine, Neil Purslow (Weigl Publishers, 2006)

Write Now! The Ultimate Grab-a-pen, Get-the-words-right, Have-a-blast, Writing Book, Joe Rhatigan, Rain Newcomb, and Veronika Alice Gunte (Lark Books, 2005)

Websites

Find out more about some scary stories and their authors:

www.shadowforest.co.uk/home
Shadow Forest by Matt Haig

www.scholastic.com/goosebumps
R. L. Stine and Goosebumps

www.roalddahl.com
Roald Dahl and his stories, both scary and funny

www.skulduggerypleasant.co.uk
Lots on the Skulduggery Pleasant series by Derek Landy

Places to visit

The Edinburgh Dungeon
31 Market Street
Edinburgh EH1 1QB

The Roald Dahl Museum
    and Story Centre
81-83 High Street
Great Missenden
Buckinghamshire HP16 0AL

The Tower of London
London EC3N 4AB

Index